The Gold Rush

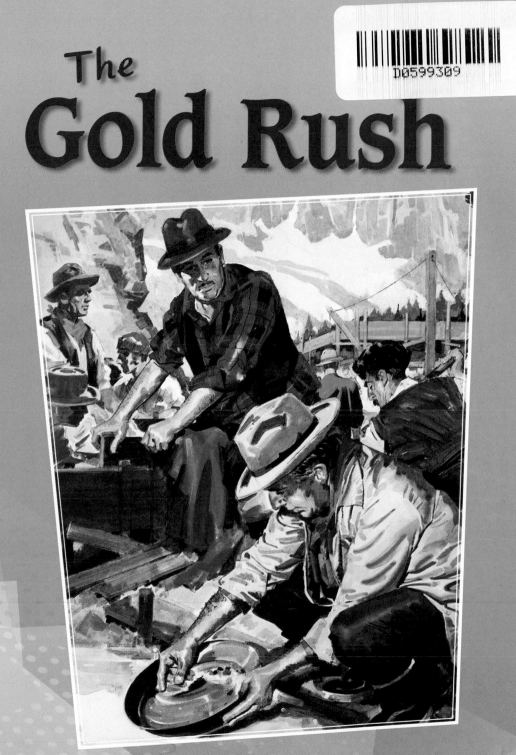

Monika Davies

Consultants

Kristina Jovin, M.A.T.
Alvord Unified School District
Teacher of the Year

Jessica Buckle
Fullerton School District

Publishing Credits

Rachelle Cracchiolo, M.S.Ed., *Publisher*
Conni Medina, M.A.Ed., *Managing Editor*
Emily R. Smith, M.A.Ed., *Series Developer*
June Kikuchi, *Content Director*
Marc Pioch, M.A.Ed., and Susan Daddis, M.A.Ed., *Editors*
Courtney Roberson, *Senior Graphic Designer*

Image Credits: Cover and p.1 Look and Learn/Bridgeman Images; pp.2–3 Ann Ronan Pictures/Print Collector/Getty Images; pp.4–5 Bridgeman Images; p.6 (inset) National Museum of American History, Kenneth E. Behring Center, Smithsonian Institution; pp.6–7, 8, 11 (top), 18–19, 21, 26–27 Granger, NYC; p.7 Hulton Archive/Getty Images; pp.10–11 MPI/Getty Images; pp.13, 29 (middle) Nancy Carter/ North Wind Picture Archives; pp.14–15 Photo Researchers, Inc/Alamy Stock Photo; p.15 (top) Creative Commons by Kaidor, used under CC BY-SA 3.0/https://goo.gl/jgHXyS; pp.16–17 Matthew Kiernan/Alamy Stock Photo; pp.17, 24, 29 (top) North Wind Picture Archives; p.20 Courtesy of the California History Room, California State Library, Sacramento, California; pp.22–23, 29 (bottom) Chronicle/Alamy Stock Photo; pp.25, 32 Universal History Archive/UIG via Getty Images; p.26 (stock certificate) Old West History Store; all other images from iStock and/or Shutterstock.

Library of Congress Cataloging-in-Publication Data
Names: Davies, Monika, author.
Title: The Gold Rush / Monika Davies.
Description: Huntington Beach, CA : Teacher Created Materials, [2017] | Includes index. | Audience: Grades 4-6.
Identifiers: LCCN 2017014103 (print) | LCCN 2017014330 (ebook) | ISBN 9781425835088 (eBook) | ISBN 9781425832384 (pbk.)
Subjects: LCSH: California--Gold discoveries--Juvenile literature. | California--History--1846-1850--Juvenile literature. | Frontier and pioneer life--California--Juvenile literature.
Classification: LCC F865 (ebook) | LCC F865 .D264 2017 (print) | DDC 979.4/04--dc23
LC record available at https://lccn.loc.gov/2017014103

Teacher Created Materials
5301 Oceanus Drive
Huntington Beach, CA 92649-1030
http://www.tcmpub.com
ISBN 978-1-4258-3238-4
© 2018 Teacher Created Materials, Inc.
Printed in China
Nordica.012019.CA21801581

Table of Contents

Strike It Rich

You are knee deep in the American River. Your hands clutch a pan. Rocks and **sediment** are piled inside. You *swish, swish, swish* the metal container back and forth, trying to shave off the top layer of soil. It's 1849. You are a miner during the California Gold Rush. You have been panning for gold for 12 hours. Your back aches. Your feet feel like ice cubes. But you keep going. You are hopeful that today is the day. Today will be the day you strike it rich.

For many Gold Rush miners, these struggles happened daily. The Gold Rush brought big changes—both positive and negative—to California. Let's take a look at this golden age in California history.

Eureka!

Have you ever looked closely at the California state seal? At the top is the state's motto, "Eureka." In Greek, it means, "I have found it." The motto refers to the discovery of gold in the state.

Civics

Gold Rush Slang

It's time to brush up on Gold Rush vocabulary! "Gold washers" (miners) worked "claims" (mines) when they were on the hunt for "the yellow heap" (gold).

Miners search for gold in rivers during the Gold Rush.

Sutter's Mill

On January 24, 1848, James Marshall was building a water-powered sawmill. The mill stood about 50 miles (80 kilometers) east of present-day Sacramento, California. Marshall had no idea he was going to play a **pivotal** role in history.

As he looked at the American River, a twinkle in the water caught his eye. It was a golden flake that glittered with promise. "It made my heart thump, for I was certain it was gold," Marshall said years later.

Oh My, Gold!

About 750,000 pounds (340,000 kilograms) of gold were mined during the Gold Rush. Most of the gold was found in flakes and small nuggets. The largest gold nugget ever found weighed 195 pounds (88 kilograms)! It was found in 1854 in Carson Hill, California.

first piece of gold found at Sutter's Mill

He showed the flake to his crew. Then, he took his discovery to John Sutter, his boss. Sutter didn't want word to get out about the gold. He knew that people would flood his land in search of more gold. It would be a disaster. The two men pledged to keep the gold a secret. But the news didn't stay quiet for long.

Sutter's Mill, 1848

Sutter's Colony

John Sutter was from Switzerland. By 1839, he was facing grim money problems. He decided to leave his home for California. Once there, he was given a large plot of land. He started a colony named *Nueva Helvetia* (NWAY-vuh hel-VEE-shuh), which meant "New Switzerland." He chose the name to honor his home country.

Word Spreads

Whispers of gold on Sutter's land grew louder. Soon, locals were mining for gold. In April 1848, Sam Brannan explored the gold mines that had sprung up on Sutter's land. He was a businessman who started a newspaper, the *California Star*. The year before, he'd also opened a store in Sutter's colony.

Brannan did not head into the mines for gold. Instead, he bought every shovel, pan, and pick axe he could find for his store. He knew miners would need supplies.

One month later, on May 12, Brannan traveled to San Francisco. He walked into the streets, swinging a small bottle of gold flakes in the air. "Gold! Gold! Gold from the American River!" he shouted.

His words sparked a **frenzy**. In weeks, many people left San Francisco. Men headed to the mines to "strike it rich." Within a few years, Brannan became California's first millionaire.

Sam Brannan

Making Millions

Brannan first opened a store at Sutter's Fort in 1847. Months later, he heard gold was found in Coloma. He opened a second store there. Some days, he made as much as $5,000. That's equal to more than $120,000 today! Eventually, he opened a third store. Brannan became one of the wealthiest land owners of his time.

Economics

The California Star

VOL. 4 **YERBA BUENA, JUNE 10, 1848** **NO. 9**

THE EXCITEMENT AND ENTHUSIASM OF GOLD WASHING STILL CONTINUES—INCREASES.

Many of our countrymen are not disposed to do us justice as regards the opinion we have at different times expressed of the employment in which over two thirds of the white population of the country are engaged. There appears to have gone abroad a belief that we should raise our voices against what some one has denominated an "infatuation." We are very far from it, and would invite a calm recapitulation of our articles touching the matter, as in themselves amply satisfactory. We shall continue to report the progress of the work, to speak within bounds, and to approve, admonish, or openly censure whatever, in our opinion, may require it at our hands.

It is quite unnecessary to remind our readers of the "prospects of California" at this time, as the effects of this gold washing enthusiasm, upon the country, through every branch of business are unmistakably apparent to every one. Suffice it that there is no abatement, and that active measures will probably be taken to prevent really serious and alarming consequences.

Every seaport as far south as San Diego, and every interior town, and nearly every rancho from the base of the mountains in which the gold has been found, to the Mission of San Luis, south, has become suddenly drained of human beings. Americans, Californians, Indians and Sandwich Islanders, men, women and children, indiscriminately. Should there be that success which has repaid the efforts of those employed for the last month, during the present and next, as many are sanguine in their expectations, and we confess to unhesitatingly believe probably, not only will witness the depopulation of every town, the desertion of every rancho, and the desolation of the once promising crops of the country, but it will also draw largely upon adjacent territories—awake Sonora, and call down upon us, despite her Indian battles, a great many of the good people of Oregon. There are at this time over one thousand souls busied in washing gold, and the yield per diem may be safely estimated at from fifteen to twenty dollars, each individual.

We have by every launch from the embarcadero of New Helvetia, returns of enthusiastic gold seekers—heads of families, to effect transportation of their households to the scene of their successful labors, or others, merely returned to more fully equip themselves for a protracted, or perhaps permanent stay.

Spades, shovels, picks, wooden bowls, Indian baskets (for washing), etc., find ready purchase, and are very frequently disposed of at extortionate prices.

The gold region, so called, thus far explored, is about one hundred miles in length and twenty in width. These imperfect explorations contribute to establish the certainty of the placera extending much further south, probably three or four hundred miles, as we have before stated, while it is believed to terminate about a

league north of the point at which first discovered. The probable amount taken from these mountains since the first of May last, we are informed is $100,000, and which is at this time principally in the hands of the mechanical, agricultural and laboring classes.

There is an area explored, within which a body of 50,000 men can advantageously labor. Without maliciously interfering with each other, then, there need be no cause for contention and discord, where as yet, we are gratified to know, there is harmony and good feeling existing. We really hope no unpleasant occurrences will grow out of this enthusiasm, and that our apprehensions may be quieted by continued patience and good will among the washers.

The Rush Is On

By 1849, news of the California Gold Rush had swept the nation. People living on the East Coast and in the Midwest made plans to move west. The westward **migration** began.

People took big risks for the chance to find gold. Workers making limited wages saw the Gold Rush as a golden ticket to wealth. But, these hopeful miners had to get to California first.

There were two ways to reach the West. The first option was to go by boat. From New York, it took six to eight months. The boat traveled around South America. People then landed in San Diego or San Francisco.

The second option was to travel over land. From the Midwest, it was a journey of about 2,000 miles (3,200 kilometers). The route was along two trails. The first was the Oregon Trail. Then, it split off to the California Trail. The trip took three to six months. Both options were difficult, but people thought they were worth the risk!

Tough Trips

The trip by sea around South America was very hard. There was little fresh water or fruits and vegetables. People often suffered motion sickness. Traveling over land took less time, but migrants had to be ready for any emergencies. There weren't many trading posts, and most people rarely had goods to trade.

Geography

Sutter's Fort to Sacramento

For John Sutter, the Gold Rush spelled his ruin. His colony was overrun with fortune seekers. Under a mountain of debt, he **deeded** his land to his son. His son then turned the land into a new settlement—called Sacramento.

AN ACCOUNT OF

CALIFORNIA,

AND THE

WONDERFUL GOLD REGIONS.

A New Arrival at the Gold Diggings.

WITH A DESCRIPTION OF

The Different Routes to California;

Information about the Country, and the Ancient and Modern Discoveries of Gold;

How to Test Precious Metals; Accounts of Gold Hunters;

TOGETHER WITH MUCH OTHER

Useful Reading for those going to California, or having Friends there.

ILLUSTRATED WITH MAPS AND ENGRAVINGS.

BOSTON:
PUBLISHED BY J. B. HALL, 66 CORNHILL.
For Sale at Skinner's Publication Rooms, 60½ Cornhill.

Price, 12½ cents.

Sacramento, 1850

Migrants poured into California. At the end of 1848, around 5,000 miners were looking for gold. In 1849, that number grew 10 times to 50,000.

The miners were called *'49ers* because of the year. They arrived in huge crowds. Most miners came from the Midwest and the East Coast. But, news of the Gold Rush reached beyond the borders of the United States. People also traveled from Europe and Asia to mine for gold.

Everyone had the same golden dream, but a **harsh** reality greeted them. The **myths** about the Gold Rush described gold lining the riverbeds. It all sounded so easy. But mining was hard work. To find gold, rocks needed to be torn up. Miners had to wade into freezing rivers. They combed through dirt. They spent hours panning for gold. Their hands became raw and bloodied. They even lost their fingernails.

How to Pan for Gold

1. Pick a location where gold has been found.
2. Fill your pan with some promising soil and rocks.
3. Shake the mixture so the gold settles at the bottom. (Remember, gold is heavy!)
4. Carefully swish the rock mixture so the top layers swirl out. (Slowly, though!)
5. Golden flakes should settle at the bottom of your pan. Eureka!

A miner pans for gold in the American River.

Changing Times

The Gold Rush changed California. But the years right before the Gold Rush were also a time of change for the state. The region had been a part of Mexico, but the United States wanted it. In 1846, the two countries went to war. They fought for two years. On February 2, 1848, they signed a treaty. California was now part of the United States.

At almost the exact same time, gold was found at Sutter's Mill. Only nine days separated these two major events! Within a few months, thousands of people came to the state. Their lives would change forever. The lives of the people who already lived in the state would change, too.

The first battle of the Mexican-American War was fought on May 8, 1846.

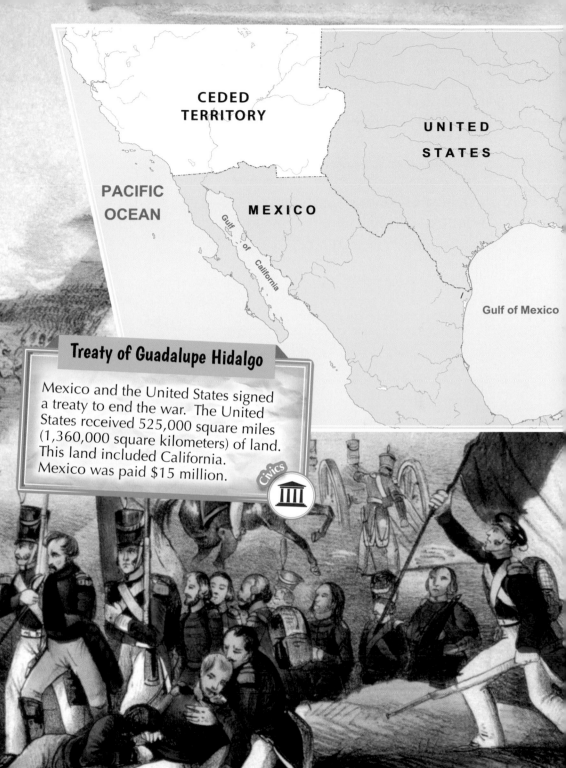

CEDED TERRITORY

UNITED STATES

PACIFIC OCEAN

MEXICO

Gulf of California

Gulf of Mexico

Treaty of Guadalupe Hidalgo

Mexico and the United States signed a treaty to end the war. The United States received 525,000 square miles (1,360,000 square kilometers) of land. This land included California. Mexico was paid $15 million.

Civics

Californios

Mariano Guadalupe Vallejo (gwah-dah-LOO-pay vah-YAY-hoh) was a Mexican leader. He came from an upper-class ranching family. There were many wealthy ranchers in the area. They were called Californios. Vallejo was in favor of the United States **annexing** his homeland. He thought it would be good for his people. Then, the Gold Rush happened. Thousands of white settlers came to the state. Californios quickly became the **minority** in their own land.

Rancho Petaluma

Vallejo founded Rancho Petaluma (pet-uh-LOO-muh) in 1834. It is still home to the largest **adobe** (uh-DOH-bee) building in the country. The ranch made most of its money from selling cowhides and **tallow**. There was also a structure to store grain and crops. The adobe building (shown above) is now part of a state park.

Economics

Vallejo had enjoyed a long career. But his name didn't protect him. He lost money and land. His ranch once was 250,000 acres. It shrank to 300 acres. The United States never paid him for his losses. He began his young life rich and strong. In the end, he was poor and weak.

After the war, Californios were supposed to be treated like U.S. citizens. Because of the Gold Rush, this did not happen. They ended up on the outside. For some miners, the Gold Rush brought riches. For other people, such as the Californios, it spelled ruin. Vallejo never got all of his land back.

Prisoner

Vallejo spent time at Sutter's Fort. But it wasn't because of the Gold Rush. In 1846, a group of American settlers rose up against the Mexican government. This was called the Bear Flag Revolt. Vallejo was held prisoner for two months at the fort.

The Chinese

Californios were not the only ones to face **discrimination**. The Gold Rush brought people from all over the world to the state. But when gold became harder to find, tensions heightened. Some white settlers felt they were **entitled** to the gold. They saw other **ethnic** groups as a threat.

Many miners were from China. At first, the other miners were curious about the newcomers. Then, more Chinese immigrants came. There was more competition for gold. As time went on, resentment toward the Chinese miners grew.

Chinese gold mining camp

In 1850, the Foreign Miners Tax was put into place. It charged miners from other countries $20 per month to work in the United States. That would be over $575 per month today. It was unfair to tax people based on their ethnicity. Many Chinese miners stopped mining. They moved to the cities. There, they set up shops. Still, many white Americans blamed immigrants for their problems.

A Safe Place

Did you know San Francisco has the world's largest **Chinatown** outside of China? It was also the first Chinatown in the United States! Chinatown took shape during the Gold Rush. It gave Chinese immigrants a safe place to feel at home.

Geography

Women in the Mines

Most migrants to California were men. Louise Clappe was one of the few women who braved the new frontier. She came with her husband, who was a doctor.

From 1851 to 1852, Clappe wrote letters to her sister back east. At the time, Clappe lived in Rich Bar, California. It was a small town filled with gold-hungry miners. Her letters paint a vivid picture of a miner's life.

Clappe described her new home as having "no newspapers, no churches, … or theaters; no fresh books; no shopping, … no daily mail (we have an express once a month); no vegetables but potatoes and onions, no milk, no eggs, no *nothing*."

Yet Clappe was happy. Her letters gave insight to her **rustic** world far from the "civilization" of the East. She wrote 23 letters in total, under the **pen name** "Dame Shirley." The letters became known as the "Shirley Letters."

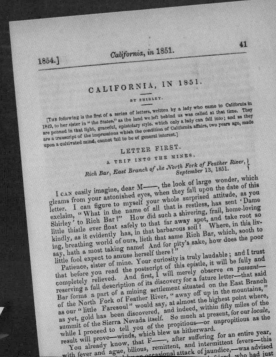

Louise Clappe's letters were printed in a magazine in the 1850s. They were later published as a book (left).

Outnumbered!

In 1850, there was a state **census**. There were a lot more men than women. More than 85,000 men were counted. But only 7,000 women lived in the state!

miners in 1852

Wilson's Bread

Luzena Wilson was **savvy** during the Gold Rush era. As one of the few women in the state, men paid top dollar for her home-cooked meals. It is said that Wilson's first sale was homemade bread that she sold for $10. That would be over $280 in today's money! That's an expensive loaf of bread!

Economics

The Changing Landscape

California became a state in 1850, and it kept growing. Within one year, there were more than 125,000 people in the state. **Boomtowns** sprung up. San Francisco burst to life. The city once was a tiny village. By 1851, eight hundred ships had docked there. One year later, the city housed over 30,000 people.

People still panned for gold. The mining scene was crowded. But there were fewer golden payouts. Most of the time, farmers' lives were better. They made more money than the miners.

Ship-tastic Lumber

Thousands of ships docked in San Francisco's harbor. But, once people arrived, they abandoned their ships. The ships' lumber was put to good use, though. Laborers used the lumber to build houses, stores, and more.

Some miners did strike **pay dirt**. In the town of Rich Bar, miners found over $23 million worth of gold. That would be worth over $725 million today!

Of course, those golden years didn't last forever. Gold mines dried up. But the cities remained. So did the migrants. Today's California grew from these early mining towns.

The Hangtown Fry

Try a Hangtown Fry! This oyster omelet is one of the first dishes invented in California. Supposedly, a man who struck it rich asked for the most expensive meal money could buy. The Hangtown Fry was born using eggs that were $1 each and oysters that were 50¢ each!

San Francisco, around 1850

Population Explosion

Immigrants suffered during the Gold Rush. Many were not welcomed. But they kept coming to the state. They crossed oceans from France, China, and Japan. They traveled north from South America and Mexico. Americans moved west, too. By the mid-1850s, 1 out of 90 Americans lived in California. Many of the people who came to find gold decided to stay. They turned to farming and other businesses.

San Francisco was one of the biggest cities in the West. It continued to grow, even when gold fever cooled. The city went on to anchor the first **transcontinental** railway. With the railroad, even more people moved west.

The state's economy boomed. Money poured into the state. Huge cities formed up and down the coast from San Jose to San Diego.

Hydraulic mining made finding gold faster.

Shaping California

The Gold Rush changed lives. It also changed the state's landscape! When "surface gold" was gone, miners turned to hydraulic mining. Jets of water scrubbed away hillsides. This altered what the land looked like—permanently.

Geography

Sheep-ish Numbers

Livestock was important during the Gold Rush. Miners craved meat! As a result, the sheep industry soared to new heights. When the Gold Rush began, there were just 20,000 sheep in the state. Over the next 20 years, the number of sheep climbed to 2.75 million!

San Francisco, around 1878

The California Dream

The Gold Rush changed California. The state's population soared. Its economy grew. Cities swelled. New towns popped up. The state would not be what it is today without the Gold Rush.

California is considered golden for other reasons. Many industries have thrived there. Farming and technology have made their marks in the state. The aerospace and film industries are also huge.

People still come to California. Some hope to get rich quick just like the '49ers. Others come to enjoy the state's beauty and climate. The Golden State has a golden origin. Its future looks golden, too.

Eureka Mining District, Nevada County, California. Ten Shares.

No. 25

CAPITAL $1,000,000.

Republic Mill and Mining Company,

Incorporated April 27, 1877. San Francisco, June 17 1905

This Certifies that H. W. Meek is entitled to Ten shares of the Capital Stock of THE REPUBLIC MILL AND MINING COMPANY, Transferable on the books of the Company by endorsement hereon and surrender of this Certificate.

10,000 SHARES $100 EA

G. S. Dyer Secretary. H. W. Meek President.

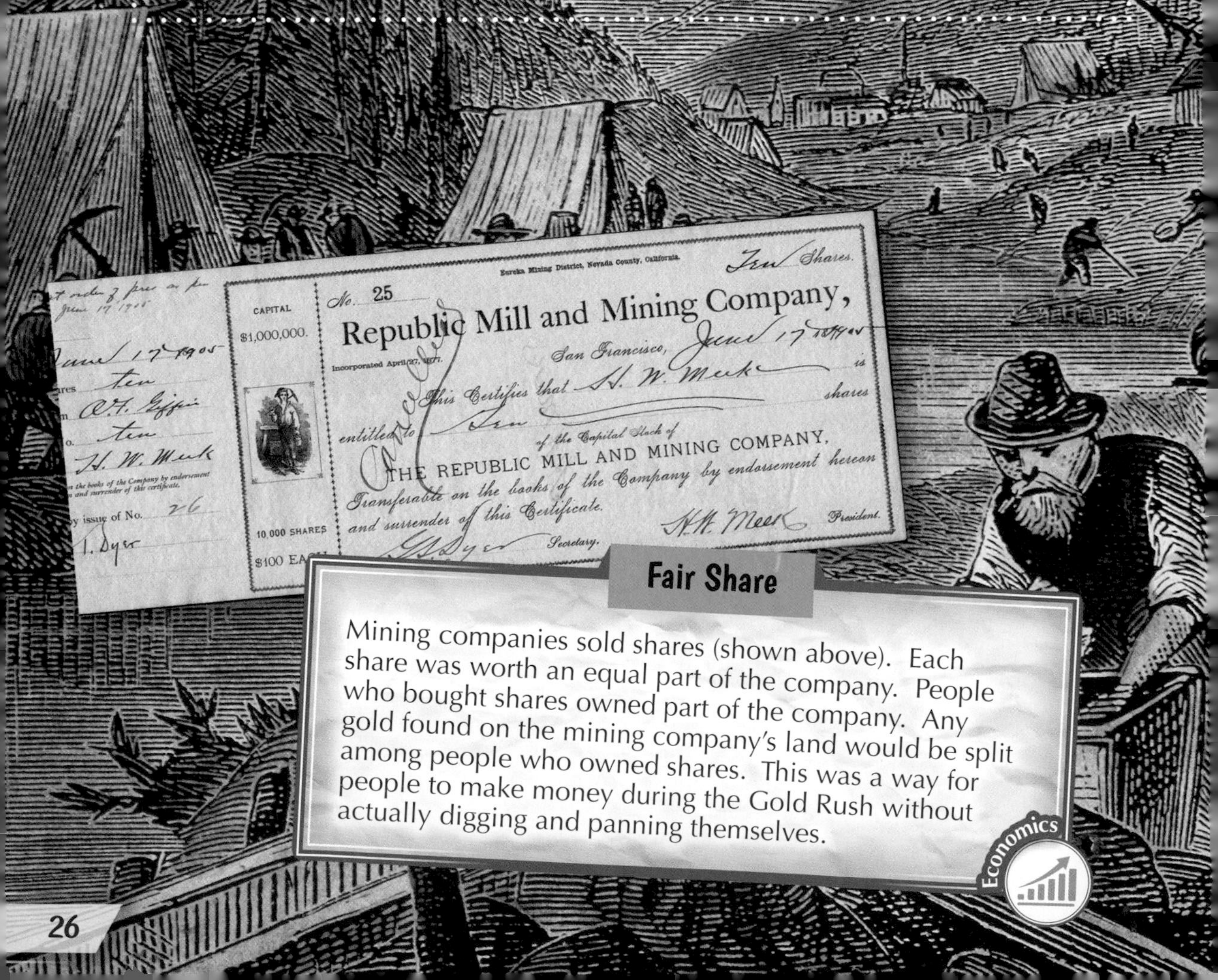

Fair Share

Mining companies sold shares (shown above). Each share was worth an equal part of the company. People who bought shares owned part of the company. Any gold found on the mining company's land would be split among people who owned shares. This was a way for people to make money during the Gold Rush without actually digging and panning themselves.

Economics

The Golden State

Most people think that the discovery of gold is the only reason for California's nickname. It has been called the Golden State for another reason as well. In the spring, golden poppies grow in fields all over the state. It was made the official nickname in 1968.

Miners search for gold at the base of the Sierras.

Write It!

You are a '49er who recently arrived in California. It's 1849, and the mining fields are pretty crowded. That only makes life more exciting—especially because you know there's gold to be found! You have been mining for a month. While there are still no nuggets of gold in your pocket, you're sure your luck will change soon.

Write a letter to your family back east. Share exciting details with them that will bring your experiences to life. Your letter might include details about the following:

- your journey to California
- conditions of the gold mines
- how much money you spend on food

- how you pan for gold
- new friends you've made
- your impression of the West

Glossary

adobe—a type of brick that is made by mixing mud and straw and letting it dry in the sun

annexing—taking an area or region and adding it to a country, state, etc.

boomtowns—towns that experience a sudden growth in business and population

census—an official count of people living in a particular place at a particular time

Chinatown—a part of a city that is mostly settled with Chinese residents and businesses

deeded—transferred property or land

discrimination—unfair treatment based on differences, such as race, gender, appearance, or age

entitled—given a right to (someone)

ethnic—of or relating to groups of people who have common cultural ties

frenzy—great and often wild or uncontrolled activity

harsh—unpleasant and difficult to accept or experience

migration—a movement from one country or place to another

minority—the group that is the smaller part of a larger group

myths—stories that are believed by many people but are not true

pay dirt—found great amounts of something after a long search

pen name—a fake name used by an author

pivotal—very important

rustic—of, relating to, or suitable for the country or people who live in the countryside

savvy—having practical understanding or knowledge of something

sediment—particles that settle to the bottom of a liquid

tallow—fat from cows and sheep, which is used to make things like soap and candles

transcontinental—going across a continent

Index

Your Turn!

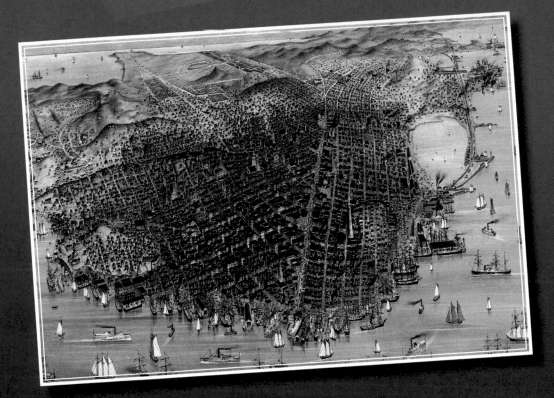

City Planner

As more people came to California for the Gold Rush, cities popped up almost overnight! Imagine you're a city planner. You get to decide where streets and buildings will be. Design a city that will serve all the people moving to the area.

Think about what people will need. Where will you place stores that sell food and mining supplies? Where will you build a hospital? What other buildings will meet the needs of this growing population?